Gérald Gambier

*"Life is not about getting there quickly,
it's about knowing how to get there"*.
La Plaisante Sagesse Lyonnaise

Courtyards & Traboules of Lyon

*I address my cordial thanks to
Annie and Régis Neyret for their attentive reading.*
Gérald Gambier

ÉDITIONS
LA TAILLANDERIE

COLLECTION PLURIEL
directed by Gérald Gambier

Text:

Gérald Gambier

Photographs:

- **Gérald Gambier:** covers, pages 4, 5, 6, 7, 9, 10, 11, 12, 13, 14, 15, 16, 17, 19, 20, 22, 23g, 24, 25, 26, 27g, 28, 29h, 30, 31, 33, 34, 35, 36, 37, 39, 40, 41, 42, 43hg, 43bg, 43bd, 44hd, 44b, 45, 46, 47, 48, 49, 50b, 51, 52, 53, 54, 55, 56, 57, 58, 59, 60, 61, 63.

- **Christian Badel:** pages 3, 8, 18, 21, 23d, 27d, 32, 38, 50h, 62.

- **Martine Leroy-Patay:** page 29b.

- **Magali Panet:** pages 43hd, 44hg.

Plans:
Patricia Brun

Infography:
PAO Concept

Correction:
Agnès Duriez

Translation:
O.E.C. Lyon - 04 78 42 35 90

© Éditions La Taillanderie - 2005
Rue des Frères-Lumière
01400 Châtillon-sur-Chalaronne
Tél. 04 74 55 16 59
Fax 04 74 55 14 27
contact@la-taillanderie.com
www.la-taillanderie.com
ISBN - version brochée français - 2-87629-261-0
ISBN - version reliée français - 2-87629-263-7
ISBN - version brochée anglais - 2-87629-264-5
ISSN en cours

Contents

▶ Why traboules ? 3
▶ A question of style 9
▶ What are the traboules ? 13
▶ Passages 16
▶ What is the origin of the word traboule ? 17
▶ Where are the traboules ? 19
▶ The layout of traboules 22
▶ How many traboules are there ? 25
▶ Stairs in the traboules ? 27
▶ The court/traboule plan 33
▶ Who do they think they're fooling ? 39
▶ Details 41
▶ Traboules and symbolism 43
▶ The literary traboule 45
▶ Some of the finest traboules 52

WHY TRABOULES ?

Some words come forth from the depths of our subconscious, shrouded in mystery; "traboule" is one of those words. It embodies Lyon's discrete, even secretive side, its dark, old passages leading to hidden courts and their myriad architectural treasures. But, above all, the traboule exerts a powerful force on our imagination, taking its source in history.

Magnificent Gothic ribbing at 11 rue du Boeuf.

Thanks to my uncle – a purebred Lyon native – who introduced me as a boy to the mysteries of the traboules, I came to imagine fine, wimple-coiffed ladies gliding across the galleries and armed knights dashing through the passages. Though my childish daydreams seemed wildly disconnected from reality, many years later I was overjoyed to learn that jousts had been a regular attraction on Rue Juiverie and that the great Bayard, the fearless and noble knight we read about in school, had triumphed at a tournament in Lyon. My youthful dreams were not so fanciful after all.

My visits with my uncle took place in the 1960s, a time when Lyon's Old City was mostly a grimy black, much as local author Henri Béraud described the atmosphere in his novel *Ciel de suie* (Charcoal Sky), and far removed from the well-groomed quarter as we see it today. Some passages were so dirty that my uncle, though a bona fide native, but perhaps not very brave, preferred to abandon any further exploration. Who might be lurking in the shadows? We get something of an idea from Charles Exbrayat, the famous detective story writer and avid fan of "*the murky atmosphere of these passages connecting the bustling and noisy streets; corridors where a discrete people live, hidden from the view of strangers*".

In sum, the traboules are a stage and the show is *The Mysteries of Lyon*.
I thank my uncle for putting me on the right path!

The traboules can be found in three different quarters of the city. Visiting them is a way to plunge into history and witness how they continue to influence the lives of the modern inhabitants. Our curiosity then becomes a solemn act of remembrance.

This is because the traboules tell the story of the humble people of Saint-Georges and Saint-Jean in the Middle Ages, when the plague and cholera ravaged the population and doctors of the Hôtel Dieu went about fumigating the passages, cloaked in great capes and black leather masks with a stork-like beak to avoid contamination. But they also tell the story of Italian and German bankers at the stock exchange and of the merchants of Saint-Paul, residents of the fine homes which are now the pride of the city. These respected citizens also used the traboules, perhaps to go enjoy a beer at their favourite tavern, identifiable in old times by a sheaf of leaves hung above the door.

*4 rue Saint-Claude.
The Croix-Rousse is filled
with perilous stairways.*

When Lyon was attacked by the Baron of Adrets and the Huguenot troops in 1562, and again when the city was taken by the revolutionary guard in 1793, firmly intent on destroying it all, many a local man escaped death thanks to his knowledge of the hidden traboules.

They also tell us of the hard-working people of the Croix-Rousse, labouring over their weaving looms and inspecting their silk fabric in the frail light of an oil lamp to look for defects that might lower its value. Yet their love of perfection and constant attention to detail did not protect the Canut silk workers from great poverty and despair, finally driving them to organise revolts, brutally crushed by the troops of Louis-Philippe in 1831 and 1834, then by those of the Third Republic in 1848.

Later in history, the traboules were also a tool for the French Resistance in Lyon which made ample use of their maze-like paths to hide their movements. We instantly think of Jean Moulin heading for a meeting of the National Liberation Committee, his face partly hidden by a scarf, or the frantic flight of liaison agent pursued by the henchmen of Klaus Barbie. The traboules were often the scene of deadly encounters but there is no doubt that this complex network facilitated the task of the freedom fighters in the *capital of the French Resistance movement*.

32 bis rue Burdeau/ 19 rue Leynaud. Plunge into an authentic Croix-Rousse traboule towards Passage Thiaffait.

Hidden behind monumental doors which perfectly symbolise Lyon's two unseemly traits – both show-offish and stand-offish – the traboules may occasionally play "hard to get" which confirms an old saying in *La Plaisante Sagesse lyonnaise* (the encyclopaedia of Lyon colloquialisms): "*If you make too much show of your wife and your money, you risk someone robbing you of both. As for getting them back, you can expect to see your wife sooner than your riches...*"

But don't give up! Your exploratory efforts will be rewarded by the discovery of superb and rare architectural elements found in a great number of passages. Lyon's Old City is replete with intriguing features; be it a suspended double vault with no central pillar, or an impost decorated with peacocks, a label stop with a sculpted figure of a portly Lyon bourgeois, a jutting grate or a stairwell banister carved directly into the stone wall; not to mention the fabulous assortment of Renaissance water wells or the ingenious

Elegant Renaissance tower at 23 rue du Bœuf.

Opposite: rue du Bœuf. Admirable galleries in the central court of Cour des Loges Hotel.

constructions of Philibert de l'Orme, already a gifted architect at the age of 26, who built a suspended court gallery supported by a single pillar only 50 centimetres wide. The spiral stairways, too, offered architects the opportunity to demonstrate their imagination and technical flair.

In the Croix-Rousse quarter, the flights of gryphite limestone in the 19th century stairways came to define a specific style found only in this neighbourhood. On this, the "working hill", the stairways are numerous and seemingly endless, plunging down the slope or suspended between two buildings or clutching onto a façade in a dizzying manner.

On the Presqu'île (peninsula), the traboules offer a medley of styles. Just walk along Quai Saint-Antoine or around the Opera House to get a glimpse of the juxtaposition of eras, sometimes found in a single building, such as 27 quai Saint-Antoine.

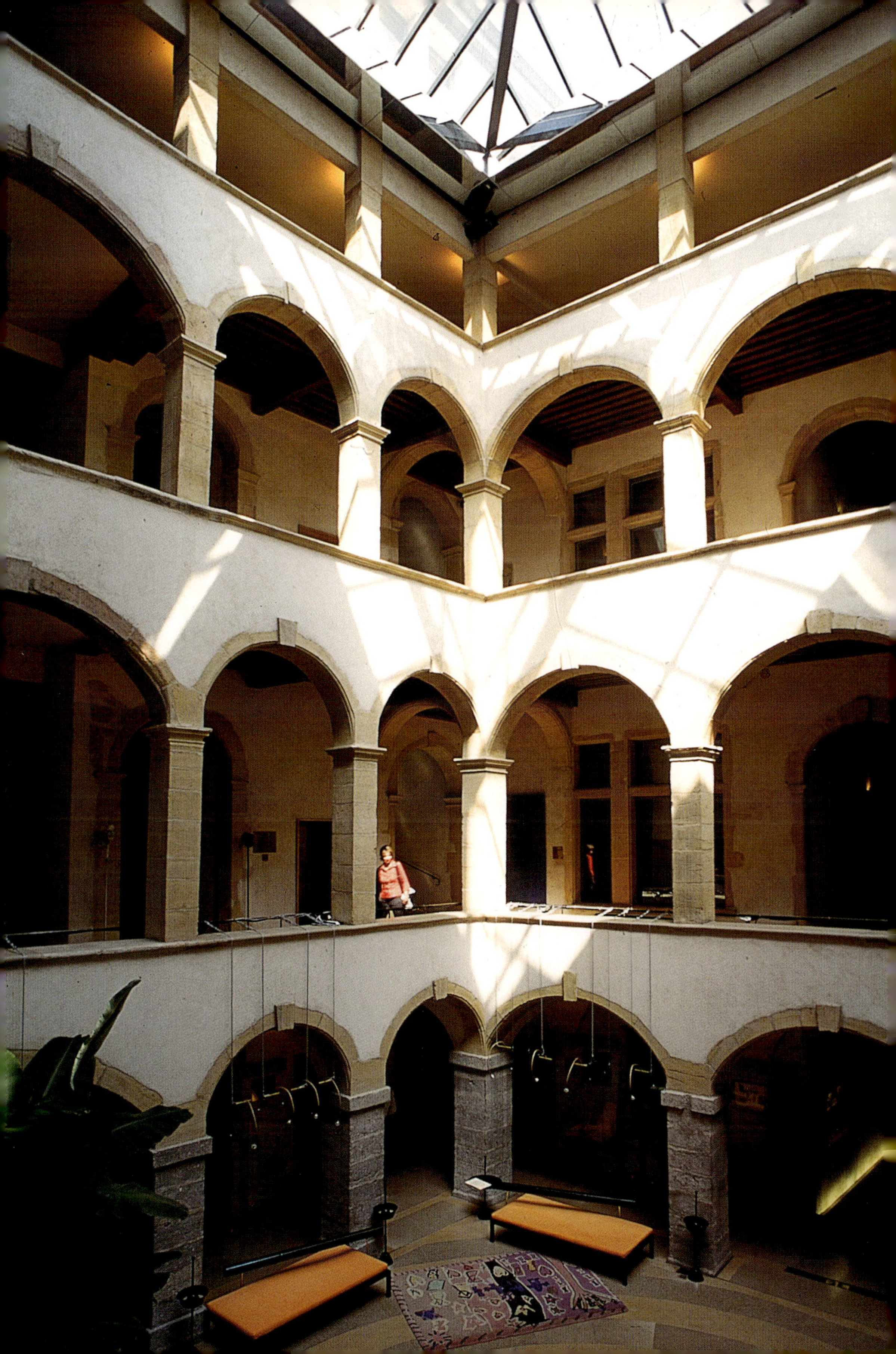

Beyond the architecture and history, the traboules are like a maze and treasure hunt combined, well plotted out by the publishers of itineraries which aim to connect two points of the city via the most secretive routes. They will be happy to learn that, in 1910, a certain Jean Robert published *Concours des Allées de Traboule* (A Race through the Traboules) about the flight of a petty thief from a crime scene on Rue Bellecour, who managed to escape the police in the Passage des Terreaux, after an exciting chase through 18 traboules.

While fully enjoying the fun or cultural side of these visits, you should also keep your eyes and mind open to the apparition of light. The soft and gentle light of Lyon which, on a particularly fine day, when it spills through the light wells formed by the courtyards, brings out the subtle grain of the stones and a delicate palette of colours. And there, like a vision, comes the enchantment of genuine beauty.

21 rue Royale/
11 quai André-Lassagne.
A traboule through a typical silk worker building.

a question of style

Many visitors to the city wonder about the architectural style or date of the buildings they see. In these pages, they will hopefully find some guidance, based on some simple elements of architecture. To properly understand, it is best to refer to the pages concerning stairways and wells, two essential features of the traboules.

Opposite: *20 rue Juiverie. 1493.*
Gothic *cross-ribbed arches in the passage.*

Below:

Left: *20 rue Juiverie. 1493.*
Double transom mullions with elaborate carvings confirm the late **Gothic** *style.*

Right: *place de la Trinité.*
Gothic *style mullions.*

The districts with traboules, Vieux-Lyon (the Old City), Croix-Rousse and Presqu'île, were built over a period of nearly five centuries, from the Gothic era to the end of the 19th century. And yet it is not always so easy to establish a simple correlation between a style and a particular period which developed the style.

As an example, the Gothic period began in France in 1118, with the construction of the churches at Morienval and Poissy, and continued to the middle of the 15th century when the Middle Ages gave way to the Renaissance. But in fact we can see major differences. The Renaissance actually began in the Italian Quattrocento period. By 1430, the Italians were already building in the Renaissance style while, in France, the flamboyant Gothic style was at its pinnacle and continued for many years more: the masterpiece of flamboyant Gothic, Brou Church in Bourg-en-Bresse, was built in the years 1503 to 1532. At the same time, in Lyon, Philibert de l'Orme was building his famous gallery, the archetype of French Renaissance style; which earned him the appointment as architect to the court of François I.

Opposite: *14 rue Lainerie. 1516. Façade typical of the* **Flamboyant Gothic** *style. Arches of the ogee windows decorated with finials and framed by pinnacles decorated with greyhounds.*

28 rue Saint-Jean. Refined cross-ribbed arches of the **Flamboyant Gothic** *style. On the second floor, the bridging and tiercerons are forerunners of the coffered shapes of the Renaissance.*

*8 rue Juiverie. Philibert de l'Orme gallery: first work by the young architect, in 1536, and archetype of the French **Renaissance** style. De l'Orme developed his concept in Lyon and soon applied it all over France, thanks to the patronage of François I.*

In Lyon, only buildings of transitional styles, Henri IV and Louis XIII, which experts classify as either late Renaissance or early classical, correspond to their actual era.

In addition, architects often employed certain new stylistic elements, without totally abandoning the use of older styles, or they might partially redesign a building with the latest style in fashion. This produced some strikingly hybrid silhouettes such as 27 quai Saint-Antoine, in the Presqu'île quarter, where we find traces of the 15th through 18th centuries, and at 37 rue Saint-Jean, with its mix of Gothic and Renaissance styles.

16 rue du Bœuf. Maison du Crible.
This magnificent bossed portal with segmented pediment presenting a nativity scene is typical of the **Henri IV** *style.*

15 rue Lainerie. Building with all the characteristics of the **Louis XIII** *style: segmented pediment and flat mullions typical of the 17th century.*

what are the traboules?

Every region has words catalogued as colloquialisms, or lexemes, which constitute local linguistic identity. In addition to the popular lingo now valiantly defended by the *Friends of Lyon and Guignol*, Lyon is the origin of two words which have entered into common usage in France and which together sum up the city: *"bouchons" and "traboules"*.

12 rue René-Leynaud.

*5 rue de la Platière.
Lovely Gothic building.*

The first of these regional terms, *bouchon*, whose secondary meaning in the Croix-Rousse quarter is a term of endearment – "*my little bouchon*" – is primarily the name given to those friendly little restaurants which have done so much for the culinary fame of the Capital of Gaul, or "Gueules" (mouths), as some would have it.

As for the traboules, the definition is not so obvious.

First of all, the word is an ondonym, i.e. a term designating a path. According to *the Larousse* dictionary, a traboule is a "*Narrow passage which connects two streets via a block of houses.*" But, more precisely, we should add that they are covered passages enabling pedestrians to go from one street to another through a block of dwellings. We'll see later that the traboule is not always a mere passage.
The Robert dictionary, complete with dates, gives an interesting detail about the origin of the word. The verb "to traboule" apparently dates from 1894, while the noun traboule came into usage in the early 20th century. The date 1894 corresponds to the first written use of the word, as published in the famous *Littré de la Grand'Côte* by architect Clair Tisseur, known as Nizier du Puitspelu, in which he asserts that the verb form "*is used only in the expression: a passage which traboules, a passage which runs through. I thought the word was simply slang, but in fact is it Lyonnais. From "tra" (trans) and "boule" (roll). A passage that traboules is a passage that crosses through…*".

Rue du Bœuf. Superb Gothic tower of the hotel-restaurant La Tour Rose, *in a former 16th century convent.*

32 rue du Doyenné. The discrete presence of this little tower gives it a southern look.

The verb "to traboule" thus predates 1894, since it was commonly used at that time, but we have to confess that we don't actually know the precise origin. What is interesting is that Nizier du Puitspelu confirms by default in this text that only the verb form existed in his day; the noun traboule is not used, and we can deduce that, contrary to the assertions of certain Lyon historians, the verb does not come from the noun, but vice versa. It was in fact not until 1905 and the little tourist guide by Antoine Rivoire, the founder and first president of the first Tourist Office, that we see the noun "traboule" in print.

This may explain the reticence of our elders to use the term, and they certainly do not use the neologism "miraboule" invented in 1961 by Félix Benoit to designate traboules open at one end only and finishing in a court where we have come to admire (from the Latin "*mirar*") the grandiose architecture which is the trademark of the miraboule.
Though the word traboule has long been sanctified by dictionaries and common usage, Lyon natives tend to use it only in reference to folklore or tourism, preferring for day-to-day use the words passage and court.

We should note, moreover, its absence from official use. With the exception of one of the most famous, the Cour des Voraces, a complex traboule with three openings, you'll find no mention of them on maps of the city.

Les passages

Passage des imprimeurs connecting 26 quai Saint-Antoine and 56 rue Mercière is a genuine traboule because it is for pedestrians only and is covered for most of its length.

Below:

Left: *passage de l'Argue is not a traboule in the historic sense of the term.*

Right: *passage Thiaffait, though very impressive, is not a traboule.*

what is the origin of the word traboule?

According to the historian and archaeologist Amable Audin, the word traboule comes from the Latin "*trans*" (through) and "*ambulare*" (to move about); which would give the verb "to traboule" the meaning "*to move through*".

In his book on traboules, René Dejean tells us that, according to the linguist André Compan, in the Langue d'Oc dialect of southwest France, a shortcut is known as "*travoulo*" or "*traboulo*". But is there really a connection? The linguistic evolution of two different regions does not necessarily warrant such a claim. The phonetic resemblance is of course striking, but the Langue d'Oc dialect is not generally associated with Lyon, which lies in the heart of the Franco-Provençal zone. This area encompassing the Rhône-Alpes and Jura regions, along with portions of the Doubs, Switzerland and Val d'Aoste, is structurally closer to the Langue d'Oïl dialects of Bugey, Bresse, Forez, Savoy and Vaud. Linguists appear to agree that it was in the Franco-Provençal zone that two series of first-group verbs were developed, based on Latin verbs ending in "are". This observation would confirm Amable Audin's theory for the Latin form "*trans-ambulare*", but the transformation cannot have been direct.

2 rue Saint-Georges. Maison du Soleil. Narrow, elliptical gallery passages, though the straight stairway is typical of the 17th century.

A comparison of the vocabulary of dialect speakers in the Franco-Provençal zone shows that the Lyon dialect was much like any other, and not, as many authors would have it, a French base interspersed with Canut slang. This dialect evolved into French in parallel with other regional dialects. Words such as "*segroller*" and "*sigroller*" (ring a bell), though they have disappeared in French, can be found in all the dialects of the zone.

In Franco-Provençal origins, we find the prefix "*trà*", meaning passage; this leads to the French word "traverser". In the entire Franco-Provençal zone, the "*traversà*" is a crosswind, coming from the west. In the Challex dialect, in Pays de Gex, the word "*tràkå*" means cross in a straight line. In the dialect of Oisans, a "*tràbùk*" (trabouc) is a passage between houses. The phonetics are undeniably close to that of traboule. So our research should no doubt focus on its regional origins, delving into the roots of Langue d'Oïl.

2 rue Sainte-Marie-des-Terreaux.
Elliptical stairway.

2 rue Terme.
Unusual square stairway. 19th century.

where are the traboules?

Old Lyon has no monopoly on traboules. They are found throughout the sector classified as a UNESCO World Heritage site. "Trabouling" is an old Lyon habit which got its start in the Saint-Georges quarter as early as the 4th century when the inhabitants of Lugdunum, short on water due to the pillaging of the lead in Roman aqueducts, began building their homes in the low-lying areas near the river. The traboules were a way to reach the Saône directly.

The development of river commerce on the Saône and Rhone provides us with a rather logical explanation. At the time, none of the rivers had constructed embankments and the height of the water fluctuated along the shore. The houses were built on immense cellars which were inter-connected. Buried under the ancient streets of the Saint-Georges quarter lies an immense subterranean network. On the Saône, the shippers deposited their goods directly in the cellars of the merchants. At the other end, the cellars opened onto the street.

The principle of the traboule was thus established and spread throughout the area in many forms over the centuries and in different neighbourhoods. Unkind critics would say that traboules epitomise Lyon's character because they combine sparing means with the local predilection for secretiveness. In the Middle Ages and the Renaissance, when Old Lyon was being built, the use of traboules became systematic because property plots were divided into strips so narrow that, in order to optimise the space, access had to be built under the structure.

5 rue Royale.
Silk merchant building.
The impost of the traboule is decorated with stained glass.

In the 19th century, when the silk industry left Saint-Georges for the Croix-Rousse, because of the height of the new Jacquard mechanical weaving looms (3.9 metres under the joist), silk makers understood the advantages of the traboules. The new buildings, especially on the slopes of Croix-Rousse hill, included many traboules to give direct access to the silk merchants, mostly located on the Presqu'île.

Though the traboules of Old Lyon and those of the Croix-Rousse correspond to quite distinct periods, on the Presqu'île we find a juxtaposition of all styles and periods. From the end of the 15th century, in the court at 2 rue des Forces, former town hall and now home to the Museum of Printing, to 94 rue Mercière, built in the late 19th century, the Presqu'île upheld the tradition of traboules. Surprises await around every corner. Rubbing shoulders with a 19th century building stands one dating back to the Renaissance, with its admirable black stone fluted door jambs and keystones of golden limestone, as can be seen in the streets Sainte-Catherine, Mercière and Sergent-Blandan.

29 rue Royale. Counterweight well. 19th century.

2 rue Saint-Georges. Well of Maison du Soleil with a stoup and candlestick. 17th century.

23 rue Sergent-Blandan / 4 rue Poivre.
Surprising stairwell resembling theatre balconies supported by columns. One of the most interesting in the Croix-Rousse.

On the Presqu'île, in the 19th century, the local penchant for discretion and inexpensive solutions is still reflected in the traboules, or in the traboule mentality, in varying forms: bistros such as the Cintra connect one street to another; in this case, Rue de la Bourse allows businessmen to move discretely to Rue Antoine-Sallès for their romantic interludes.

A Lyon habit, you say? Definitely! But the traboule concept spread beyond the city to a certain degree throughout the region. There are traboules in Saint-Étienne, magnificent examples in Villefranche-sur-Saône, in Trévoux and a few as far away as Bourg-en-Bresse. Some even claim that the "*trajes*" of Besançon are traboules. Though there are indeed a few genuine traboules in Besançon, the *trajes* (or *trages*) are meant to accommodate horse-drawn coaches, and can also be found in the bourgeois homes of the 6th and 3rd districts of Lyon, but no one here would ever think to call them traboules.

the Layout of traboules

The layout and complexity of traboules demonstrate the practical genius of the people of Lyon.

First, there is the simple passage, a corridor with ribbed arches which, in Old Lyon, allows you to go in a straight line from the street to a court or another street. Then there is a flurry of more or less elaborate designs. Take the traboule at 54 rue Saint-Jean which cuts through the block with relatively few detours, but on the way you will cross four courts and four successive buildings before coming out at 27 rue du Bœuf. Then there is the traboule of the Hôtel du Gouvernement (2 place du Gouvernement), where you change levels twice to pass over the former stables and then emerge onto Quai Romain-Rolland.

Amongst the different types of multi-entrance traboules we often see a radial layout with a central court, mostly found in the Croix-Rousse and Presqu'île.

As with many things in life, there are record-breaking traboules. The champion of them all connects Rue Auguste-Comte (33, 35, 37) and Rue des Remparts-d'Ainay (21, 23, 25) by no less than six entrances and crossing through three buildings. Others run through four buildings, like the one with three entrances at 5 rue Auguste-Comte and 5 and 7 rue François-Dauphin.

3 rue Romarin.
Silk merchant building.
Stairwell with six levels resembling theatre balconies.
Connects to 5 place du Griffon.

In general, this type of traboule belongs to a bourgeois residential building or small factory of the 19th century, and has a coach entrance. This form tends to be rejected by purists who insist that the authentic traboule is purely pedestrian, relegating the others to the category of mere passages. The sloppy habit of calling any passage or tunnel a traboule has resulted in a regrettable amalgam of the Lyon traboule, the Besançon *trajes* and the *viols* of Die. So the question remains: are the Passage de l'Argue, Passage des Imprimeurs and Passage Mermet to be counted as traboules? Not at all! clamour the purists; they are simply passages because they do not run under the building structure. It is high time to stop misleading the tourists because it is bad for the reputation of the real traboules.

As for the multi-level traboules, they sometimes stretch to extremes. For example, you can no longer take Passage des Gloriettes which connects Rue Joséphin-Soulary to Montée Bonafous and Rue Justin-Godard because it had to be closed following a landslide, but with its long passage and 128 steps, it is still considered the longest traboule in Lyon.

Honourable mention goes to the passage joining 2 montée du Gourguillon to 35 bis montée du Chemin-Neuf: it crosses four buildings and three courts and climbs three stairways for a total of 172 steps – the equivalent of nine storeys – and ends on a path of some 40 metres.
We begin to understand how this complexity served a useful purpose during some of the city's more violent periods of history.

*4 rue Désirée.
Typical Canut silk worker
building with stairwell
in the court.*

*33 quai Saint-Vincent.
Unusual stairwell.*

Rue Terme.

*Rue Romarin.
The building takes up the entire block.*

how many traboules are there?

The first person to try to answer that question was René Dejean, in his book *Traboules de Lyon*. He catalogued 315 traboules, but he pointed out that he had purposely left out the most famous in order to devote himself to the description of other passages worthy of interest.

14 rue René-Leynaud. Opposing stairwells in a Canut building.

10 rue Sergent-Blandan/ 7 rue de la Martinière. Splendid wrought iron galleries of the 17th century at the bottom of the slopes of the Croix-Rousse.

A recent detailed inventory, complete with historic and modern maps and even aerial views, gives us a count of 215 in Old Lyon, 163 on the slopes of the Croix-Rousse, 130 on the Presqu'île and a dozen on the plateau of the Croix-Rousse, i.e. a total of more than 500 traboules connecting over 230 streets.

Based on our earlier discussion of what does and does not qualify as a traboule, should we then include the generally neglected radial passages of the left bank? They cross through square buildings much like those in the Croix-Rousse and Presqu'île, built at the same time as the Prefecture, in the middle of the 19th century.

Stairs in the traboules?

When you come down, come up and see me! exhorted Mère Cottivet, a symbol of the tough and spirited women of the Croix-Rousse, never at a loss for words, confirming that Lyon is a city of stairs: those in the street that take you up the hills, and those linked to the traboules of buildings, since every central court systematically contains one or two stairwells. So what she means, in fact, is, "*When you come down the street stairs of the Croix-Rousse, come up the building stairs to my apartment.*"

This local feature drew the attention of Rabelais who, during his stint as a doctor at Hôtel-Dieu, described in his story Gargantua the stair towers of Lyon where, after a long climb, one would find the stables at the top of the building. Only someone with intimate knowledge of Old Lyon's topography could have described it so well.

4 rue Juiverie. The enormous core of the stairway in Maison Henri IV is hidden behind a Renaissance façade.

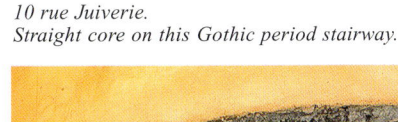

10 rue Juiverie. Straight core on this Gothic period stairway.

Rabelais was writing in 1534, a cornerstone date for three periods of construction in Old Lyon: High Gothic is still used here and there, while Flamboyant Gothic is nearing its end and more and more buildings have adopted the Renaissance style. And yet tradition still confers a key role upon the stairway at the centre of the building.

During the Gothic periods in Old Lyon, stairs were built in a spiral. Depending on the whim of the architect or the owner, we find three types of spiral staircases: stairs with a central core (post) or stair stringer, stairs with a staggered stair stringer and those with no core.

The most commonly found is the type with a central stair stringer. Some of them are magnificently constructed: at 22 rue Juiverie, 24 rue Saint-Jean (Grand Palais). Others have an exceptionally large core such as the one at the Henri Quatre mansion, rue Juiverie, and at 40 rue Saint-Jean where it is enormous and flat. Others are full of whimsy, such as 9 rue Saint-Jean, with its twisted core which splays into a palm-leaf shape under the vault at the top.

*9 rue Saint-Jean.
Exceptional spiral core.*

9 rue Saint-Jean. In the Flamboyant Gothic style, it is not unusual to see stair cores fan out under the vault into a beautiful palm tree shape.

5 place du Petit-Collège. Stairway with four curved cores by Joachim Van Risamburg. 1731.

The stairs with a staggered stair stringer are among the most audacious. They are sometimes mistakenly described as stairs without a core. The finest are located at 10 rue Lainerie, but another good example is in the Scève home (11 rue Saint-Jean), built in 1516 in the Flamboyant Gothic style for a well-to-do local family.

At 18 rue Saint-Jean, a genuine stairway without core, set in a rounded corner of the court, gives a clear view from bottom to top.

18 rue Saint-Jean. Genuine stairway without a core built into a rounded corner of the court. Modifications date from the Renaissance.

In the Middle Ages, stair rails often consisted of a torus carved into the wall of the stairwell tower or in the core of the stairs (9 rue Saint-Jean, 2 place du Gouvernement, 10 rue Lainerie, 24 rue Saint-Jean). Occasionally, corner pieces are sculpted as a reinforcement in the curve of the tower, under the longest steps (18 rue Lainerie, 44 rue Saint-Jean).

During the Renaissance, we see the emergence of stairs with the first flight of steps built straight and the remaining flights in a spiral, as at 27 rue Saint-Jean or 2 bis montée du Change. At the same time, the steps grew wider, bringing more light into the stairway.

Not much later, during the reign of Louis XIII, we see more use of straight steps, alternating with landings, as at 5 place du Gouvernement, behind the immense façade with pediments. This configuration is the precursor of standard square-cut stairs, such as those found at the Grands Carmes convent, at 4 rue de Thou, built in the 17th century.

10 rue Lainerie.

Above:
vertical view of the core.

Below: *stairway with staggered stringer. Note the banister carved directly into the wall and the core. The view from the top is positively dizzying.*

This technique reached the height of its art in what is now the 5th district government office, where the architect, Joachim van Risamburg, built a stairway with four curved cores in 1731, a foretaste of the style soon to be widely found in the Canut buildings of the 19th century.
Architects turned their attention and imagination to the Croix-Rousse quarter where they rivalled each other in the use of inventive and daring designs for the flights of steps and landings.

*4 rue de Thou/Cour des Moirages.
Former convent of the Grands Carmes.
Magnificent 17th century square stairway.*

6 rue des Capucins.
Unusual stairway alternating
straight and curved flights of steps.

29-30 quai Saint-Antoine.
Triangular flights of steps in passage B
of the Pères Antonins court. Former entrance
to the Guignol Theatre of the Neichthauser
family, located in the chapel of the Antonins
religious order, known as healers and the first
firemen of Lyon.

the court/traboule plan

Not all traboules are accessible, unfortunately. The unfettered passage of numerous visitors has resulted in damage and other nuisances which have led many owners to close off access to non-residents. In many cases, they have done this despite pocketing public subsidies for renovation work on the traboules.

18 rue Saint-Jean.
Finely reworked Gothic court.

The town authorities decided to take action. Knowing the historic and aesthetic value of this heritage resource, especially since Lyon's listing as a UNESCO World Heritage site, and well aware of the problems caused by excessive tourism, the City developed a plan in 1990 to set guidelines for restoration and establishing rights of passage. The court/traboule plan has provided for the restoration and opening of famous traboules such as the ones at 54 rue Saint-Jean and 8 rue Juiverie. The plan has been improved over the years and clearly defines the terms and mutual undertakings of the City and building owners, in order to ensure access for visitors. In 1994, the second version of the plan called for the City of Lyon to contribute financially to restoration works, specifying in greater detail the commitments of the owners.

Since May 2004, the third version of the plan sets the City's contribution at a flat rate of 70% for restoration and lighting. The City and the Greater Lyon Urban Community handle part of the cleaning and maintenance costs, including the removal of large rubbish and graffiti. In consideration for this contribution, the owners must promise to make the traboules accessible to the public every day from 7am to 8pm in the summer and until 7pm in the winter.

This latest version allows the City to set up tourist site markers. But one of the main objectives is to steer tourists towards the other sites in the Presqu'île and Croix-Rousse quarters, in the hopes of stemming the tide of visitors to Old Lyon.

*16 rue Juiverie.
Ruelle Punaise was
an open-air sewer and
a short-cut to Montée
Saint-Barthélemy.*

9 place Colbert/14 bis montée Saint-Sébastien.
Cour des Voraces, also known as Maison de la République.
Most picturesque traboule in Lyon with its six-storey façade stairway.
Scene of the Canut silk worker revolts in 1831 and 1848.

*27 rue Saint-Jean/
6 rue des Trois-Maries.
Magnificent Renaissance
court with typical stairway.*

Since 1991, over 30 agreements have been signed between the City and owners, including 16 in Old Lyon, 14 on the slopes of the Croix-Rousse and one on the Presqu'île. Nine courts were opened to the public in 2003 and 2004. Another 20 are in the works, with 15 of them on the slopes of the Croix-Rousse.
Each successive city government has worked to encourage the signing of new agreements to help enhance Lyon's heritage and make it accessible to all.

▶ traboules covered by city agreements

The figures in parentheses after the address correspond to the district and to the year in which the agreement was signed.

Old Lyon
8 rue Juiverie (5th) (1991);
16 rue Juiverie (5th) (2001);
21 rue du Bœuf (5th) (2002);
27 rue du Bœuf/54 rue Saint-Jean (5th) (1991);
2 place du Gouvernement/10 quai Romain-Rolland (5th) (1997);
32 rue du Doyenné (5th) (2002);
12 rue Saint-Jean (5th);
18 rue Saint-Jean (5th) (1998);
26-28 rue Saint-Jean (5th) (1992);
27 rue Saint-Jean/6 rue des Trois-Maries (5th) (1996);
33 rue Saint-Jean (5th) (2005);
42 rue Saint-Jean (5th) (1993);
50 rue Saint-Jean (5th) (1999);
58 rue Saint-Jean (5th) (1994);
26 quai de Bondy (5th) (2002);
3 place du Change (5th) (2001);
10 rue Mourguet (5th) (2001);
10 rue Lainerie (5th) (2002);
5 place du Change (5th) (2005);
42 montée Saint-Barthélemy (5th) (2005);
7 rue Saint-Georges (2005).

3 bis petite rue des Feuillants/5 place Croix-Paquet/Rue Lorette. Cour des Moirages.

Croix-Rousse slopes
9 place Colbert/14 montée Saint-Sébastien/29 rue Imbert-Colomès (1st) (1995);
1 rue Sainte-Marie-des-Terreaux/6 rue des Capucins (1st) (1995);
6 place des Terreaux/12 rue Sainte-Catherine (1st) (1996);
22 rue Bouteille/rue Sergent-Blandan (1st) (1996);
2-4 rue des Pierres-Plantées/5-7 rue Jean-Baptiste-Say (1st) (1996);
Cour du Moirage/4-5 place Croix-Paquet (1st) (1997);
11 rue des Pierres-Plantées/Venelle des Pierres-Plantées (1st) (1997);
20 rue Imbert-Colomès/55 rue des Tables-Claudiennes (1st) (1997);
3-5 boulevard des Capucins/6 rue René-Leynaud (1st) (1998);
30 et 32 bis rue Burdeau/19 rue René-Leynaud (1st) (1999);
5 rue Coustou/22 rue des Capucins (1st) (1999);
13 rue des Capucins / 14 rue René-Leynaud (1st) (2000);
118 montée de la Grand'Côte/7 rue Terme (1st) (2001);
4 rue de Thou/5 petite rue des Feuillants (1st);
4 rue Désirée/7 rue du Puits-Gaillot (1st).

Presqu'île
9 rue Laurencin/Cour des 3 passages (2nd) (2001).

*27 rue du Bœuf/
54 rue Saint-Jean.
Inner court of
the long traboule.*

who do they think they're fooling?

Though court/traboule agreements have been signed with the owners of these buildings with traboules, don't forget that these buildings are residences and common decency requires that we do not disturb their peace and their living environment. The plan does not give visitors the right to do as they please. This is all the more true in traboules which have not signed agreements.

On the other hand, visitors who come to see Lyon's traboules, bringing in welcome income for the tourism industry, should be directed to genuine historic traboules and not some nondescript passage between houses or gardens. Does Lyon need to scrounge for traboules to pad out the list?

Though Old Lyon may occasionally be overrun with tourists and though it makes sense to point them in the direction of other sites around Lyon, this must be done with care.

2 place du Gouvernement.
Left:
gallery..
Right:
renaissance well with shell-shaped canopy and row of pearls.

Similarly, if a building is demolished, it is only natural that passage rights consecrated by centuries of habit be preserved in the new building. But there is no reason for the new passages to be covered by these special agreements, because they certainly don't qualify as historic traboules.

Several addresses on the list of court/traboule agreements are unworthy of the name "traboule" and should be removed from the list. The credibility of all traboules is at stake:

– 9 rue Laurencin/Court of the three passages (2nd) (2001);
– 22 rue Bouteille/Rue Sergent-Blandan (1st) (1996);
– 2-4 rue des Pierres-Plantées/5-7 rue Jean-Baptiste-Say (1st) (1996);
– 11 rue des Pierres-Plantées/Venelle des Pierres-Plantées (1st) (1997).

In addition, some owners, despite the agreements they have signed and the advantages they have obtained, regularly shut off access to visitors. These include 6 place des Terreaux/12 rue Sainte-Catherine (1st) (1996), where the inner court is closed and the neighbouring bar uses it for storage space, and 10 rue Mourguet, which is always closed.

37 rue Saint-Jean.

58 rue Saint-Jean. Renaissance with triple openings and triple shell canopy.

Details

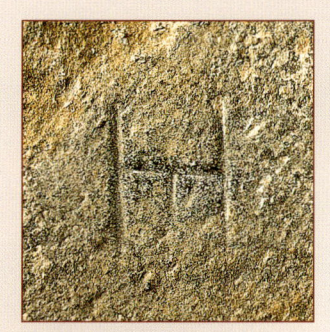

Stonecutters' marks.

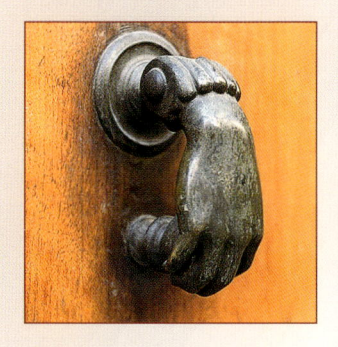

Door knockers in original shapes.

*3 place du Change.
Is there a traboule behind every door in Old Lyon? In this case, it's a finely reworked court.*

*14 rue du Bœuf.
Magic and daring of the Renaissance: arches without supporting pillars.*

16 rue Saint-Jean. Impost decorated with squirrels.

12 rue Saint-Jean. Impost with peacock.

9 rue Saint-Jean. Impost with jutting grate and peacock decoration.

4 rue de Thou. Coats of arms in the stairwell.

22 rue Sergent-Blandan. 17th century door and impost with inscription paraphrasing Cicerone: "It is not the master of the house, but the house of the master." In this case, the 19th century master was the explorer Charles de Chavannes, companion of Savorgnan de Brazza.

traboules and symbolism

At the end of the Middle Ages, the builders of the Gothic era were still influenced by Romanesque, or early Medieval art and its symbolism. This can be seen in the sculptures decorating the caps of ribbed arches or dripstones of the windows. Though it is not uncommon to find effigies of various characters such as monks, bourgeois and young women, a few buildings stand out for their enthusiastic use of symbolic and allegorical animals. Two of these are worth noting in detail.

At 18 rue Lainerie, the leitmotiv of the building is the confrontation between good and evil. In the stairwell, the first two corner pieces represent an angel and a dragon. Then you must rise, both in the physical and spiritual sense, moving past evil and arriving on the first storey where four ribbed vault caps represent the tetramorph of the Apocalypse (Jean IV, 6-7-8), that is to say, a symbolic representation of the four evangelists: the lion for Saint Mark, the eagle for John, the angel for Matthew and the bull for Luke. On the second floor, the caps represent male caryatids holding up the sky. And on the third floor, the sculptures remind us that overcoming one's weaknesses is a necessity. One cap represents a man capturing a basilisk, a symbol of evil and debauchery.

18 rue Lainerie. In the stairway, a corner piece representing a dragon, suggesting that to rise up spiritually, you must rise past evil.

53 rue Saint-Georges. Bas relief gives its name to the street. According to the Golden Legend, *Saint Georges came to Silene in Libya where a dragon threatened to destroy the people if they did not regularly sacrifice young girls to him. Though entire armies had failed to kill the dragon, Saint Georges succeeded with only his holy cross and lance.*

22 rue Juiverie. Lovely sculpture of a young girl in the portal arch.

32 rue Tramassac. Two nude women in the streets of Old Lyon; what does it mean?

2 place du Gouvernement. A griffon, symbolising obstacles to be overcome, glares at another symbol...

2 place du Gouvernement. ...the mermaid and her bewitching song.

At 2 place du Gouvernement, on the façade of the Hôtel du Gouvernement, the window dripstones have caps with mythical animals. On the gateway caps, there is a mermaid on the right and a dragon on the left: the mermaid symbolises all that attracts man, be it a beautiful woman or wealth, and turns him away from his duty. The dragon watching her symbolises the obstacles to be overcome. We can assume that these two sculptures, at the entrance to an inn, were not chosen at random.

Left:
3 place du Change. A spiral symbolising the infinite, or the head of a bird?

Right:
*18 rue Lainerie.
A man capturing a basilisk, symbol of evil and debauchery..*

the Literary traboule

You would think that our mazes of stone would be considered a prime location for filmmakers seeking the proper atmosphere for a mystery story. But you would be wrong.

Only three or four films have made use of the traboules, out of hundreds made in the region. This, in the city where the movie camera was invented. Thank heavens for literature, which compensates for the cinematographic deficiency.

Some authors, such as Jean Reverzy, in *Le Passage*, and Flora Tristan, in *Tour de France*, describe covered passages but do not explicitly mention traboules, so we will not include them in our list.

Two novels, *La Traboule*, written in 1958 by Ferdinand Breysse, and *Traboules*, by C. Berger, published by Thot (2002), use the word in the title. Guignol, the local hero (a puppet character akin to Punch and Judy), spent his fictional life in the traboules; and yet we had to wait until 1987 for the puppet play by Jean-Guy Mourguet, *La Traboule du diable*. As for comic books, it wasn't until 1992 that *La Traboule de la Géhenne*, by Yvan Delporte and Will, published by Dupuis, made use of the term.

29-30 quai Saint-Antoine. Convent of the Antonins religious order (1650). Sculpted door of the former Guignol theatre.

Thanks to another comic book, from the Léo Loden series, by Carrère and Arleston, published by Soleil Production, entitled *Kabbale dans les traboules* (1999) and a novel by Ewan Blackshore, published by G. de Villiers, *Le Guignol sanglant des traboules* (2002), our mysterious passages finally play a central role.

In a different literary genre, Bernard Clavel starts his *L'Homme du Labrador* in Lyon, in a disquieting, foggy atmosphere: "*Vague silhouettes occasionally appeared in the foggy distance, lit by the reflection on the water and the glow filtering through the dark curtains of a few windows. Here and there, a song from the radio would waft out from a traboule.*"

Charles Exbrayat, in his story *Le Chemin perdu*, takes his hero through the traboules to participate in a worker revolt by the Canut silk weavers in 1834, and then again to escape the army sent in to crush the uprising: "*Tired of the killing, the soldiers slept. Nicolas cut through the traboules that the army had no knowledge of, or could not control due to a lack of men.*"

Roger Sauter, in *Terres vives*, in 1973, played with their meanderings: "*Daytime here is but the flipside of mystery and the passages, punctuated by porches, open themselves to the dance of monsters and gargoyles. […] Under the gables, knots of traboules, treacherous steps, and twisted Gothic doors give us a sign.*"

For Bernard Siméone, in *Passages vers le centre*, written in 1984, traboules are like the inner life of the writer: "*While the words dig down, another twisted path closes in the city, a sketch of views obstructed by blind walls, inscribe in the stone the lost quest for the centre. The traboule quarter evokes so*

29 rue Royale.
The gallery allows you to circumvent the lower court.

*22 rue Juiverie.
Maison Baronnat (1446).
Galleries with
"basket-handle" arcades.*

precisely the inner landscape that writing seems to seep from it. I walked all around looking for a woman I had never seen."

In December 1942, Louis Aragon and Elsa Triolet came to Nazi-occupied Lyon. In her *Préface à la clandestinité*, Elsa Triolet describes the scene: "*On the quays, homogenous buildings with flat façades, genuine repositories of heritage, fortunes hidden in the coal grime and abandoned old walls with silk and velvet in their bellies, a narrow and twisted city, like the secret of its traboules, tragic like the water of the Rhone and Saône, and their drowned-dead, the detritus, the navigation and the bridges arching over it.*"

Opposite:

At the top:
*29 rue du Bœuf.
The Canut buildings of the 19th century in the Croix-Rousse strangely resemble 17th century buildings in Old Lyon.*

At the bottom:
*5 rue Joseph-Serlin.
Court with unusual convex walls. Connects to 2 place Louis-Pradel.*

The same Elsa Triolet, in *Les Amants d'Avignon*, sets the scene in Cour des Voraces: "*The traboule that Juliette took seemed to resolve its mystery in a great square court; in the middle of the court rose a stairway […]; giving the impression of a prison, of despair.*"

Henri Béraud, a native son, tells us that he used to "*hang out*" in all the quarters of the city. And yet in his books, traboules are few and far between. He generally calls them "*allées*" (passages), as in *Ciel de suie* (Charcoal Sky), in which he mentions "*l'allée des Veuves*".

In his *Le Mémorial de la rue Sainte-Hélène*, written in 1919, Béraud pays due homage to the traboules: "*My parents lived on Rue du Port-du-Temple, at the corner of Place des Jacobins… It was, as far as we were concerned, an admirable quarter, an old quarter, quiet and picturesque, filled with narrow streets, hidden spots and embankments. This area has magnificent traboules, peopled with black gates and dark corners, which filled our childhood with an insatiable passion for adventure.*"
But he wrote his finest lines about the traboules at the end of *La Gerbe d'Or*, in 1928: "*The 'traboule' passageways took us to the heart of an old district, full of noisy misery and revolting smells. A smell unlike any other, the odour of the land of the Canuts, the worn-down stone, flowing wine, rotten fruit, urine, petrol, hot butter – a concoction of smells, street by street, from the Terreaux to the top of the hill, reaching up to the sky.*"

6 rue des Capucins / 1 rue Sainte-Marie-des-Terreaux.

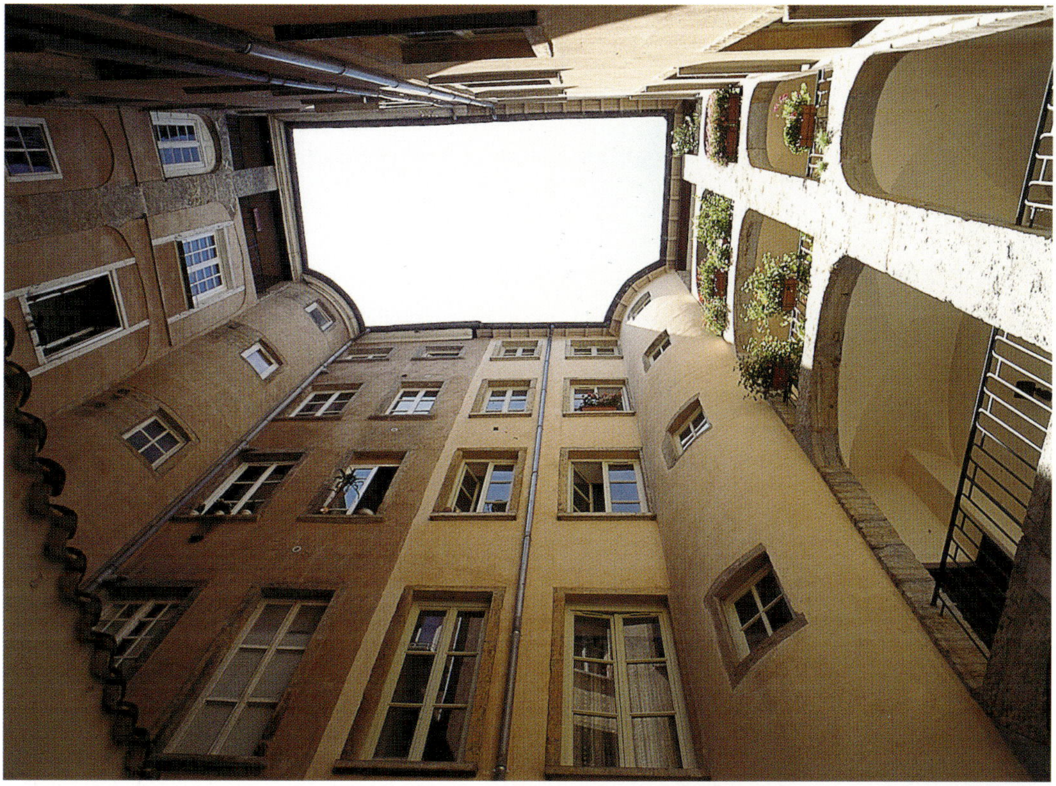

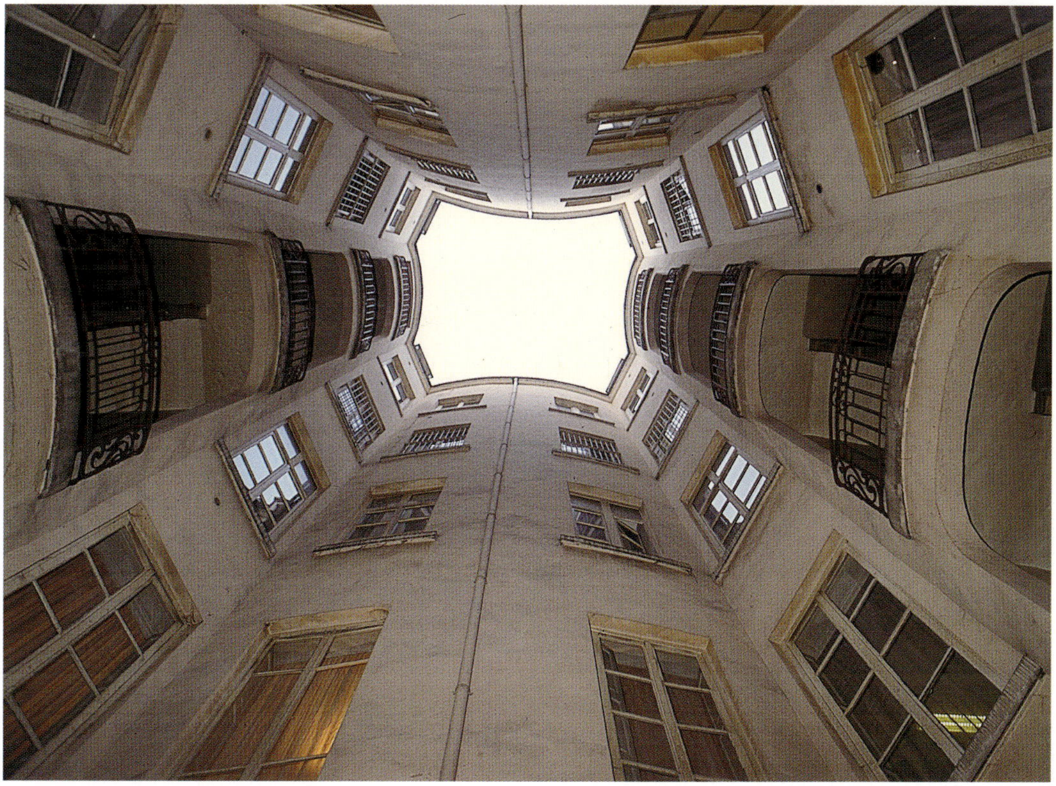

Last but not least, in the poetry of Monique Clavaud, a painter and poet, in the Lyon tradition of women poets:
"*Even the traboules which pour
Like rivers of stone swallowing up the light
to speak its secrets…*"

We can only hope that traboules continue to inspire writers who experience their splendour, mystery and poetry.

Opposite:
*23 rue Juiverie.
Stairway built in 1647.*

Right:
*52 rue Saint-Jean.
Renaissance stairway with wide steps.*

Below:
*21 quai Romain Rolland/19 rue des Trois-Maries.
Exceptional wrought iron of the 17th century;
Lyon's craftsmen were widely renowned.*

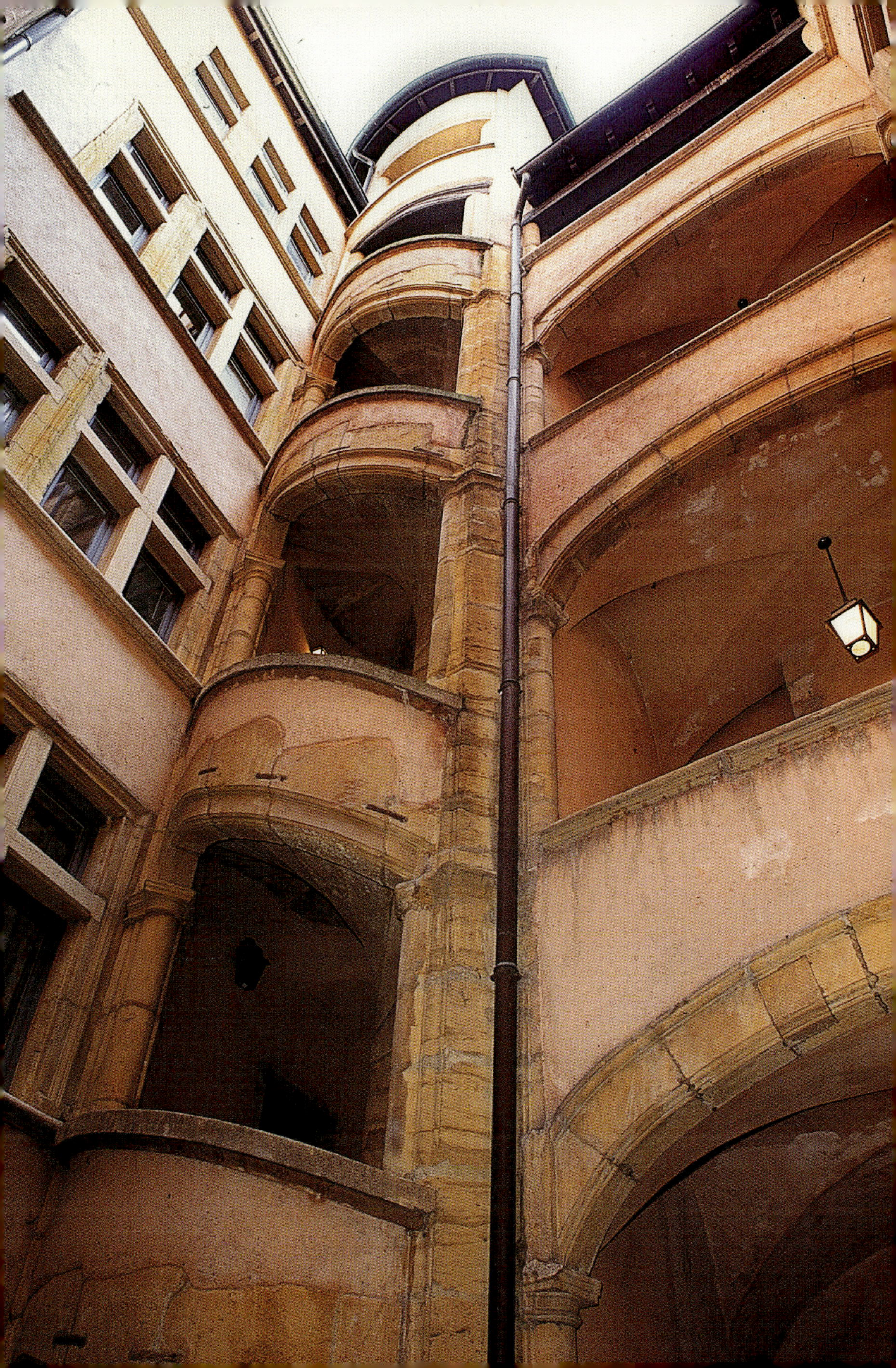

some of the finest traboules

▶ saint-georges quarter

2 rue Saint-Georges: maison du Soleil. On the corner of the building, statues of the Virgin and Saint Peter. Between them, the sun alludes to the 18th century owner, Barou du Soleil. The helmeted head on the impost refers to the 17th century owner, a captain of the town militia. Inside, an extraordinary stairwell circles around the elliptical court.

2 montée du Gourguillon: an interesting traboule, its galleries symmetrical with the stairwell; sculpted caps under the dripstones. Connects to Montée du Chemin Neuf via three stairways totalling 172 steps, three courts and a 40 metre corridor.

32 rue du Doyenné: pretty little court, the circular tower gives it a southern look.

12 rue Fernand Rey. Superb grates and balustrades of the 17th century.

*14 rue du Bœuf.
Daring and imagination
of the Renaissance.*

▶ SAINT-JEAN QUARTER

21 quai Romain-Rolland/19 rue des Trois-Maries. Exceptional ironwork from the 17th century.

14 rue du Bœuf. Hôtel Croppet. (1467). Look for the scowling character on the arch of the door.
The vaulted passage to the court consists of two semi-circular arches with central pendent decorated with a coat of arms. The stone string is decorated with a Grecian-style frieze. The gallery is closed by mullion windows framed by little semi-circular bays with arch stones. The semi-octagonal tower, with an inset column on the front face, is supported in a strange fashion at ground level, by the rear wall only and the three pillars of two rampant arches which act as a sort of squinch.

16 rue du Bœuf. Court. The Pink Tower. Bossed portal and pediment designed by Serlio, a Bolognese architect. Mid-16th century. Well with a shell-shaped canopy dating from the Renaissance.

19 rue du Bœuf. Court. Maison Outarde d'Or. 1487. In the court, at the end of the passage, a textbook example of Gothic architectonics. The galleries date from the 16th century.

5 place du Petit-Collège. 5th district government hall. Built in 1731. Stairway with four curved cores with steps of uncoursed stonework.

2 place du Gouvernement/10 quai Romain-Rolland. Built in the 15th century next to the Governor's residence, this Gothic building was an inn until the mid-19th century. On the façade, the mullions and ribs have dripstones decorated with mythical animals on the caps. Past the gate, against the left wall, there are vestiges of a coffered wood portal of the Saint-Christophe Inn of the 17th century. A loggia hangs over the stairway to the inner court. The banisters are carved into the wall. The court, raised above the stables, is a feast of Gothic and Renaissance styles, including the well with a shell-shaped canopy.

9 rue Saint-Jean/8 quai Romain-Rolland. 1516. This building marks the transition from Flamboyant Gothic to the Renaissance. With impost, jutting grate and stone string decorated with dragons. Cross-ribbed vaults in the passage with keystones. The twisted core of the stairway splays into a palm-leaf shape under the vault at the top. The galleries have two "basket-handle" arches supported by a central pillar with pinnacle. The junction at the central cap of the arch is a masterpiece of stonecutting and joining.

18 rue Saint-Jean. Hexagonal court with two sets of facing galleries with double arcades. An exceptional helical stairway without a core, in a rounded corner of the court. In the passage, keystones with coats of arms and caps with sculpted figurines, including a portly bourgeois. In the centre, an arcade with balusters from the 17th century.

23 rue Juiverie.
A unique building with bossed façade of 1647.
Late Louis XIII style moving toward the classic age.

27 rue Saint-Jean/6 rue des Trois-Maries. Sumptuous building of the late Renaissance. On the façade, joined casement and mullioned windows with fluted pilasters and pediments. Raised arches of the boutiques decorated with keys. At the entrance to the court, a turret supported by a squinch. Magnificent spiral stairway after the first straight flight of steps. Rectangular tower with semi-circular double arches and inclined entablature supported by inset pilasters. Groin-vault galleries and "basket-handle" arches.

28 rue Saint-Jean. Court from the late 15th century, with two facing towers and galleries. The crossed ribs of the galleries are simply extraordinary. They illustrate the exuberance of Flamboyant Gothic and give a preview of the Renaissance style to come. On the first floor, they twist around a circle of three lobes decorated with daisies; on the second floor, they divide into lozenge-shaped ribbing with coats of arms.

37 rue Saint-Jean. Maison du Chamarier. The Chamarier was an ecclesiastic noble and one of eight dignitaries of the cathedral's chapter house. In charge of the police and court of justice in the grand cloister, he was the keeper of the keys to the fortifications. He collected taxes during the fairs.
This Renaissance building was made by order of Chamarier François d'Estaing in the late 15th century, near Porte Froc of the ramparts. The court has an extraordinary water well.

27 quai Saint-Antoine. Three eras in one place: 18th century façade, Renaissance cross-ribbed vaults, 15th century court Flamboyant Gothic (16th c.) galleries with "basket-handle" arches. Skylight and well with shell-shaped canopy.

*Impasse Sergent-Blandan.
Unique stairway with ogee landings.
Upper timber frame takes
the same shape.*

*118 montée de la Grand'côte/7 rue Terme.
A genuine Coix-Rousse traboule with long
corridor and stairway.*

42 rue Saint-Jean. Court. Lovely 15th century façade with hollow mullioned casement windows. Projecting turret. The mullioned windows of the court have colonnettes. The galleries open onto the court with double "basket-handle" arches which become semi-circular moving to the top. Exceptionally wide stairway.

50 rue Saint-Jean. Court. Semi-octagonal tower, galleries with low vaults supported by finely decorated console caps.

52 rue Saint-Jean. Home of the printer Guillaume Leroy, associate of the master printer Sébastien Gryphe. Spiral stairway in an exceptional round tower of the mid-15th century.

54 rue Saint-Jean/27 rue du Bœuf. A maze of passages under four buildings and through four courts. The last two courts are separated by stairs with dual support of the core and an elliptical column. The openings have rampant arches on one court and low arcades on the other.

58 rue Saint-Jean. One of the finest Renaissance wells in Old Lyon with three openings topped by shell-shaped canopies. The friezes shown under the arcade were discovered under a plaster coating in one of the rooms.

3 place du Change. The Gothic stairway is not in a tower but in a rounded corner of the court.

60 rue Saint-Jean/Rue de la Bombarde. Maison des Avocats. Built in 1516 on the site of the former Croix-d'Or Inn, founded in 1471, whose only vestige is the coach portal. Acquired by the Lyon Bar Association in 1979, an audacious restoration plan enhanced the exceptional façade and its three levels of galleries. The building is now the International Museum of Miniatures.

▶ saint-paul quarter

3 place du Change. Beautiful Gothic court. Spiral stairway. On the left, mullions with colonnettes, on the right, double hollow mullions. At the foot of the corridor arch, a strange animal with twisted eyes.

10 rue Lainerie. Magnificent spiral stairway with staggered stair stringer. Note the banister carved directly into the wall and the core.

18 rue Lainerie. Fine vaulted passage with cross-ribbed arches ending in caps with angels, devils and animals. In the spiral stairway, eight sculpted corner pieces. The caps in the galleries are decorated with symbolic sculptures: a tetramorph (4 evangelists) (1st floor); male caryatids (2nd floor); a man capturing a basilisk (3rd floor). Stairs supported by a surprisingly large column.

60 rue Saint-Jean. Maison des Avocats. Built in 1516 on the site of the former Croix-d'Or Inn (1471). Acquired by the Lyon Bar Association in 1979, restoration works enhanced the exceptional façade and its three levels of galleries. Now home to the International Museum of Miniatures.

42 rue Saint-Jean. Mullions with fine colonnettes and groin-vault arches in the galleries (16th century).

4 rue Juiverie/Montée Saint-Barthélemy. Hôtel Paterin, known as Maison Henri IV. Built circa 1550. Partly destroyed during the enlargement of Montée Saint-Barthélemy in 1863. Façade rebuilt in 1734. Exceptional building with a spiral stairway twisting around an oversized core, three levels of galleries with semi-circular arcades. On the left, a Renaissance niche under a double segmented pediment shelters a Madonna. On the right, a bust of Henri IV. The wheel pump and ornamental basin date from the 17th century.

2 rue des Forces/13 rue de la Poulaillerie. Museum of Printing. Former Hôtel de la Couronne and town hall of Lyon. Superb court dating from the late 15th century, displaying a reproduction of the Claudius Tablets.

8 rue Juiverie. Hôtel Bullioud. In the first court, a well topped with a shell-shaped canopy. In the second court, a gallery commissioned by Antoine Bullioud in 1536, designed by Philibert de l'Orme, a young Lyon architect only 26 years old at the time. De l'Orme was given the task of connecting two buildings via a gallery but without encroaching on the rather small court and without demolishing the existing well. He designed a loggia buttressed by two turrets on squinches which transfer the weight to the side walls and a single central pillar. Decorated in Greco-Roman style, the two storeys combine the Doric style below (alternating fluting) and Ionic above (capitals with volutes). The turrets are topped with triangular or curved pediments. The interior is decorated with frescos and Latin mottos. Stonecutter's mark on the vault jamb.

23 rue Juiverie. Maison Dugas or Maison aux Têtes de lions. Built in 1647. Long bossed façade and semi-circular arcades, highlighted with 15 lion heads. Flat mullions typical of the 17th century. The Madonna in the corner is from the same period. In the court, a two-sided well, French stairway with semi-circular core but straight flights of stairs.

▶ PRESQU'ÎLE

29-30 quai Saint-Antoine/64 rue Mercière. Antonins Court. A surprising double structure on the stairs in passage B.

27 quai Saint-Antoine/58 rue Mercière. Overlap of 15th to 18th century styles. Renaissance well with small aedicule. Lovely sculpted caps in the passage.

2 rue des Forces/13 rue de la Poulaillerie. Former Hôtel de la Couronne (15th century) which was the town hall in the 16th century. Renaissance court. Now the Museum of Printing.

*16 rue du Bœuf.
Pink tower with staggered windows,
formerly had a crenelated top
(16th century).*

*22 rue Juiverie.
Maison Baronnat. Projecting turret
(15th century).*

*3 rue du Bœuf.
17th century building with stairway supported by enormous stone pillars and wooden balustrades.*

▶ CROIX - ROUSSe

118 montée de la Grand'Côte/7 rue Terme. Genuine passage with two beautiful flights of stairs and inner court with four small wrought iron balconies.

Impasse du Sergent-Blandan/10 rue Terme. Ogee (S-curved) landings. Timber frame takes the shape of the ogee under the roof.

10 rue Fernand-Rey. 17th century. Sumptuous wrought iron work.

9 place Colbert/14 montée Saint-Sébastien/29 rue Imbert-Colomès. Cour des Voraces. Site of the Canut silk worker revolt in 1848.

20 rue Imbert-Colomès/55 rue des Tables-Claudiennes. A fine Croix-Rousse traboule with two passages, stairs and rounded cobblestones.

6 rue René-Leynaud/3-5 rue des Capucins. Traboule with two inner courts.

17 rue René-Leynaud/30 bis rue Burdeau. Louis XVI building. Magnificent traboule, long and steep stairs, leading to Passage Thiaffait. Picturesque with its rounded cobblestones, its old fountain and three levels.

5 rue Coustou/22 rue des Capucins. Genuine corner traboule with two inner courts including one with rounded cobblestones.

1 rue Sainte-Marie-des-Terreaux/6 rue des Capucins. Genuine Croix-Rousse court.

6 rue des Terreaux/12 rue Sainte-Catherine. In this passage, 80 Jews were arrested in 1944.

4 rue de Thou/3 bis petite rue des Feuillants/5 petite rue des Feuillants. Former convent of the Grands Carmes. Magnificent square stairway of the 17th century.

*10 rue Lainerie.
The tower of the stairway with staggered stringer has wide Renaissance steps.*

BIBLIOGRAPHY

- Bayard (Jean-Pierre), *La tradition cachée des cathédrales*, Éditions Dangles, Saint-Jean-de-Braye, 1990;
- Bertin (Dominique), Clémençon (Anne-Sophie), *Lyon et Villeurbanne*, Guide Arthaud, Paris, 1990;
- Boucher (Jacqueline), *Présence italienne à Lyon à la Renaissance, du milieu du XVe à la fin du XVIe siècle*, L.U.G.D., Lyon, S.D.;
- Dejean (René), *Traboules de Lyon, histoire secrète d'une ville*, Éditions Le Progrès-J. Honoré, Lyon, 1988;
- Duraffour (Antonin), *Glossaire des patois franco-provençaux*, Éditions du C.N.R.S., Paris, 1969;
- Fornas (Félix-Pierre), *Le symbolisme dans l'art roman*, Éditions la Taillanderie, Châtillon-sur-Chalaronne, 1997;
- Fornas (Félix-Pierre), *Le bestiaire roman*, Éditions la Taillanderie, Châtillon-sur-Chalaronne, 1998;
- Gouttard (Marie), *Les Madones de Lyon*, Éditions La Taillanderie, Bourg-en-Bresse, 1991;
- Jacquemin (Louis), *Guide de Lyon et la Courly*, Éditions La Taillanderie, Bourg-en-Bresse, 1989;
- Jacquemin (Louis), *Le vieux Lyon*, Éditions La Taillanderie, Bourg-en-Bresse, 1995;
- Jacquemin (Louis), *Traboules et Miraboules*, Éditions La Taillanderie, Châtillon-sur-Chalaronne, 1999;
- Neyret (Régis), *Guide historique de Lyon*, Éditions du Tricorne, Genève, Éditions Lyonnaises d'Art et d'Histoire, Lyon, 1998;
- Nicolas (Marie-Antoinette), *Le Vieux-Lyon, Old Lyons, 5 circuits*, Éditions Lyonnaises d'Art et d'Histoire, Lyon, 1995;
- Pacaut (Marcel), *Guide du Lyon médiéval*, Éditions Lugd, Lyon, 1995;
- Pelletier (André) et Rossiaud (Jacques), *Histoire de Lyon*, Éditions Horvath, Le Coteau, S.D.;
- Perrin (Raymond), *Lyon, paroles et regards*, Éditions La Taillanderie, Châtillon-sur-Chalaronne, 2001;
- Renaissance du Vieux-Lyon (ouvrage collectif), *1946-1996, 50 ans de Renaissance du Vieux-Lyon*, Lyon, 1996;
- Renaissance du Vieux-Lyon (ouvrage collectif), *Lyon, un site, une cité, Le livre du Site Historique, Patrimoine mondial de l'Unesco*, R.V.L., Lyon, 2000.

- Le Journal de la *Renaissance du Vieux-Lyon*;
- *Lyon Cité*, revue municipale de Lyon;
- *Lyon Citoyen*, revue municipale de Lyon;
- Journal *Le Progrès*.

Achevé d'imprimer en avril 2005 - dépôt légal 2e trimestre 2005
Printed in U.E. sur les presses de Beta